Table of Co

Foreword

Sharon Cooper

PSS is a social care charity that works across the UK and in the Isle of Man. We have one key purpose: to help people get the most from life, whether that's about supporting them to make their family stronger, improve their health and well-being, get out and about in the community or find a safe and happy home. In 2019 our organisation will celebrate its 100th birthday, but even as the years mount up one thing's for sure, we're not slowing with age. At PSS, we believe in encouraging people to choose their own support. To make this a reality we provide a range of services which work across a wide spectrum of personal experience and need.

Our Women's Turnaround service supports women who are involved with the criminal justice system, to help reduce reoffending. We do this by offering group work, one-to-one support, practical and emotional support and counselling in a safe environment. Our aim is to work with the women we support to look at root causes of their offending behaviours – and often we find we're working with women with multiple and complex needs; including domestic abuse, substance misuse, housing issues, mental health problems and family issues, to name a few. We work with a wide range of women who very often have not had the support they've required and have ended up within the criminal justice system. Our aim is to support the women to make better-informed choices, improve their wellbeing and make life changes to make their future a positive one.

Our Ruby service supports females who have experienced domestic abuse. The women we work with in this service receive intensive support from our specialist team. A number of the women we work with as part of our Ruby service also use our Women's Turnaround service, and so were part of the group working with Writing on the Wall to produce this book.

Behind every woman we work with is a story. These women share their lives with us and often their lives are have not been straightforward or easy. Some women have made unwise decisions, but accessing the support at Women's Turnaround enables them to learn, make changes and empower themselves to take an alternative road in their lives. This book captures some of these stories and gives an insight into some of the journeys these women are on.

I would like to say a big thank you to all the women who have opened up and shared their lives and stories. I'd also like to thank my teams for encouraging the women to attend, especially Lisa Irvine who's determination ensured women turned up to the writing sessions! I'd also like to say thank you to Writing on the Wall and Margy McShane for delivering the sessions and making this book possible.

The things you will read are not easy but they are real life and from real women who have the right to have their stories told. When we asked them for their feedback at the end of the writing process, one woman wrote: **'...it helped me put my thoughts into words. I'm sad it's ended – it's been amazing.'**

I hope that when you read this, you will be amazed too!

Sharon Cooper,
PSS Service Manager

Introduction

Emma Hulme

'No offence but...'

I've learnt a lot over the past twelve weeks working with PSS and Women's Turnaround. I've learnt we readily give a voice to some women and forcibly silence others. I've learnt that sometimes we have to face ourselves and sometimes we have to ensure other people face us, making sure they really see and hear us. But most importantly I've learnt that there is no force like the coming together of women.

I'm always questioning what it means to be a woman but these women have all been defined and stereotyped in a notoriously male dominated environment. An environment by were simply being female means they receive harsher sentencing than their male counterparts or are left to rebuild already shattered lives from the bottom up, over and over again.

Women within the criminal justice system often have children who are left behind if they are incarcerated. They are thirty times more likely to self-harm than the general public, with 1 in 4 doing so. 53% of women in prison report to having suffered emotional, physical or sexual abuse. It's no good punishing women without looking at why they are in this situation to begin with. The stigma and shame attached to women who have a criminal record forbids them from moving forward with their lives and it's time that changed.

This book is an honest, raw and joyous account of stories about childhood, loss, family and addiction. It's an account of women at their worst but also at their very best. And honestly, these were some of the most inspiring women I have ever had the privilege of working with.

I need to say a huge thank you to all the staff at PSS, in particular Lisa Irvine, without whom this project would not have been possible. To Margy McShane who led us all on this wonderful journey and Jenny Newman for helping the group to edit their work. However, my biggest thanks and congratulations are reserved for the group. They bared their souls and for that I will be forever grateful.

Enjoy.

Emma Hulme,
Programme Manager, Writing on the Wall

No Offence

Heartbreak Husband

Andrea Davies

Going out to the garden was the best escape for Anne to get away from sounds of whistles and men shouting at the TV. Taking her washing basket and pegs with her, she hummed along to 'Love Me Tender' - one of her favourite songs from The King as she hung her clothes out to dry on the warm sunny afternoon.

At the age of 77 (or 21 every year as Anne likes to claim), she had always fantasised about marrying Elvis. But once the fantasy ended came the reality of being married to her childhood sweetheart of 52 years - John. A wonderful man who tried to make her fantasies come true by styling his hair, curling his lip and doing The King's famous grunts.

It took her a while to realise it, but the humming had slowly turned into a rhythmic guitar. 'Is that a real guitar? That can't be me making those noises.' Speaking aloud caused the birds in the garden to look at her like she was losing the plot. Anne decided she had to find where the beautiful music was coming from.

Shuffling down the twisty path in her slippers, towards the back of the garden, she found herself completely confused as to why her bin-shed was having its own concert. Snapped out of her trance by the sound of a frog coming from the pond, she leant over to make sure it was okay and caught her own reflection in the water. Twenty-one every year was no longer a wish - the reflection looking back at dear Anne was indeed her twenty-one year-old self.

The bin shed door swung open, Anne spun round and was dumbfounded at the sight that met her eyes. 'Oh bejesus, what do you think you're doing in the bin shed!' were the only words she got out before passing out on to the grass, legs up in the air and slippers gone awry. Waking up to a strange mouth trying to blow life back in to her felt like someone had pressed the puff up button on a puffer fish until the realisation of just whose air it was she was breathing. And swiftly with no delay she grabbed the back of his neck and turned the mouth-to-mouth into a full-on snog...

Picking twigs and leaves out of her hair, The King told Anne how he had waited in her bin shed for an opportunity to be alone with her so he could ask for her hand. All her fantasies where coming true but what about her lovely Elvis-impersonating husband?

Well maybe if she kept him fed and watered she could keep visiting The King in the bin-shed and keep him safe for those days when she needed to do her washing… But for right now it was back to reality to tell her husband the same thing she had told him for years: 'Elvis ain't dead cause I heard him on the radio.' Or in Anne's case in the bin shed.

A Word With The Sky

Andrea Davies

Friendship is something that very often gets taken for granted. Having or being a best friend can sometimes be a very daunting task that comes with a lot of expectations, responsibilities, promises made not to be broken and the shame that comes with letting a loved one down.

If you're lucky you can always be forgiven with time but a harder thing to earn is to forgive yourself. I let you down. I broke promises. I didn't meet my expectations. But, most of all I didn't take responsibility for my actions. It may be too late to earn your forgiveness now, but I think at last I've started accepting my own.

I will never forget what I did but I have learnt from it and one promise I can make to you now, that won't be broken, is that it will never be repeated.

Brothers

Andrea Davies

Strong hearted brave joy
Beautiful love pain my boys
Memories given

Spider-Man figures
My cheeky monkeys laughing
The sound of happy children

Brothers together
One just a babe one a boy
So, grown up yet still so young

Kisses on little heads
Let me tuck you in tightly
Goodnight my sweet peas

Katrina The Dragon

Andrea Davies

Katrina my girl, what can I say but I'm sorry? You didn't deserve to go out like that but imagine how it felt for a nine-year old to discover that overnight her dog had ruined a great friendship and taken away her adventure buddy!

You were pink and fluffy and the best for a cuddle, my prized possession. You came everywhere with me and I treated you like part of the family. From being fed tea and toast that just made your mouth soggy to having your own seatbelt in the car, so you were safe. Getting bubbly in the bath at bath time and guarding all our treasures at night whilst I slept. My lovely pink dragon with your purple spikes on your back and the glow in the dark star on your chest.

How I miss picking berries, making magic potions with you and fighting the evil mushroom imps that live amongst the fungi at the bottom of the apple tree. That fateful morning - oh I remember it well - walking out into the garden ready for our next mission only to see your purple toes sticking up out of the mud with my Doberman lying next to her accomplishment, so proud, whilst fluff hung from her teeth. Pulling you out of the ground, thinking I could give you a wash, was the worst mistake after realising all I was holding was a fluffy thigh. Traumatised is not even the word!

I'm also sorry to admit that three weeks later I moved on to a purple monkey - but in your honour, I named her Katrina number two.

Perfectly Imperfect

Andrea Davies

With your olive coloured skin
With your finger nails bitten too short
With your crackly bones
With your laugh that can be heard for miles
With your smell so familiar and relaxing
With your decisions made so rashly
With your eyelashes to be envied
With your big fat nose
With your hopelessness thinking
With your painful moods and anxiety
With your overgrown beard and the caterpillar that lives on your lip
With your lovely calm patience and self-restraint
With your temper tantrums that could make a two-year old blush
With your promise to be the best you can be as long as you're near to me

The Magic Box

Ashley Crookall

I will put in the box:
The smell of a coconut cloud
The silence of a drum kit
And a pink kitten that barks when he is afraid

I will put in the box:
A love letter from a leprechaun
A three-piece bathing suit
And a dizzy iguana

I will put in the box:
Sensual strawberry kisses
Four stolen moments
And a giraffe with wings

My box is cherry, charcoal and circular
Etched with coffee and vanilla lilies;
Spanish wishes in each corner
I will cradle my box under the black stars of a scarlet sky
Like a pot of rainbow, no gold to be seen

Friday Fright Night

Ashley Crookall

Friday arrives, yet again. For many, the anticipation of the weekend also arrives. Whatever the plans may be for the weekend, a few social drinks with friends, cherished moments with a loved one, household chores or just being able to relax, unwind and put the working week to bed. Once you're out the office door, you're free.

Not for me. Leaving the office did not leave me feeling free. My stomach churns, my walk home erratic. For me it is less about anticipation and more about fear, I knew what was coming.

These fears will be quashed once I make that call. I nervously pick up the phone, overcome with desire and doubt. Maybe if I didn't make that call, tomorrow could be a good day. I always make that call. It was by no means a heartfelt, thought evoking conversation; a simple 'Hi Ash, be down now' and that was that. He would likely be the only person I spoke to until work on Monday.

There is one stop to make before home, I need supplies. Cigarettes, some red wine (maybe even a bottle of Prosecco in case I want to bask in the bubbles), a puzzle book (the inner geek in me wants my mind occupied) and of course, candles, just to set the mood.

The wait for him feels like a lifetime. The obsession unbearable. 'Why am I being kept waiting' I wonder, 'I'm good to him, I should be a priority'. I check my watch and check my phone (as if the two would tell me a different time) what is it they say, 'a watched pot never boils'. Stupid phrase, I don't want pot, or even hot water.

Manically, I change my bedding, hoover and clean my already spotless room. I take that back; my room is not a bedroom; it is a luxury prison cell of my own making. I phone him back, a little of what dignity I have left eaten up in those contracted minutes, 'I'm on my way Ash'.

Gut wrenching anxiety consumes me, where the hell is he on his way from, Liverpool is not that big a city. Take a deep breath, it's not even six pm, the night is still young (what does that even mean). I pace the floor, unable to sit with myself, there is too much at stake.

The phone rings, I barely contain a squeal of excitement. Dammit, it's not him. I ignore the call; I don't have time for chit chat at an important time like this. The phone rings again, the vibrations against my desk deafening. Yes, finally he is here.

As I skip down the stairs, keys and money in hand, a feeling of relief takes over. It's not quite the Cadburys Crunchie Friday feeling, but I admit 'I'm so excited' (thanks Pointer Sisters).

Our encounter is brief, just how I like it. Less than a minute, but a minute too long. I race back up the stairs, fist clenched, guarding the expensive gifts I have just bought for myself. Despite the impatience I experience during my ridiculously long wait (half an hour at most), I have some final preparations to see through. I shower, dry and straighten my hair. Adorned in my best lingerie, I take a sip of the red wine; the deep, dark fruit flavour warms my insides. I light my candles, vanilla scented flames flicker. The mood is set. A quick cigarette to calm my nerves and I begin. I carefully open one of my gifts. I must be gentle, I am dealing with a delicate, hand tied wonder here.

I empty the contents on to my desk and as a wave of nausea hits me I separate the wondrous white substance into evenly sized and evenly spaced lines (I'm a Virgo, I strive for perfection). Armed with my precisely cut straw, I bend over. What a release. This is what I've waited for all day. I shudder, a cold chill down my spine and a tingle in my fingertips, a wave of momentary peace, intoxicating gratification.

I get into my fresh, warm bed. Pencil in hand (ink is too much of a commitment) and eagerly open this week's 'Puzzler'. Where to start: Sudoku, Crossword, perhaps even a Code word. It doesn't make much difference, I'll plough my way through many of the brain-teasing challenges. After all, the night is still young (ah, I get it!) I reward myself after each completed puzzle. A grip of smug satisfaction takes hold, next line, next cigarette and then back in bed.

Time goes by so fast, yet almost too slow. Fuzzy head and wine stained lips. This is not healthy me-time, this is soul destroying isolation. Don't listen to the head, this is normal. Where else would I possibly be, where would I even want to be. I don't have time to be around people, they will either get in my way of my Russian roulette routine or God forbid, want to share what I've got.

This cycle goes on through to the early hours of yet another Saturday. I'm all out, that's fine, you've had a good night (honest), why not just go to bed. The internal demon inside me, let's call it a 'little coke gremlin' (sounds cuter) tells me it's not enough. More, More, More (you speak a True word Andrea).

I check the time, should I, shouldn't I, can I, can't I. I do, I make that call. Man, number two, come on down. This time I'm told half an hour, that's cool, a man who tells it straight, he's a good guy (albeit someone who is equipping me with tools to cease, each line leads me closer to a slow and painful death).

I take a look in the mirror and grimace with despair. With shaky hands and blurred vision I apply make-up. The realisation of how shocking I actually do look becomes apparent. I slather on layer upon layer of foundation. Mask after mask until I give up. No amount of face paint can deny this disaster. I slip into something a little less comfortable, old faithful, little black dress and wait. I carry out this insane process for two reasons, firstly to conceal the truth, pretend like I've had a great night out with friends and that we're just on carrying on the party for a while longer (and not that I am pathetic, weak and lonely) and secondly, I don't want him to know that I've bought from elsewhere (I can be loyal).

As I wait, the gut-wrenching anxiety returns. Yet again I pace the floor, yet again I check my watch and my phone. Calm down you lunatic, he'll be here when he's here. Suddenly, as if he's manipulated his way into my mind, he phones (there's a connection for you). He's here!

It's less of a skip down the stairs this time and more of a tiptoe. Levels of regular function compromised. I get into his flash car (so that is where some of the money goes!) and we both avoid eye contact. That suits me just fine. Thank you very much and off we go.

Once back in my bedroom, I undress. Both myself and the bag. I'm just going to have one and then I will save the rest for tomorrow, it'll save me having to leave the house. Honestly, I will just have one. My inner little grem disagrees. It's never just one, now that it's here it would be awfully rude to leave any behind.

And so, my night continues. I lay there alone, in silence and in deathly darkness, the candles haven't survived the night, but will I? Mind racing and heart beating. Thump after thump, I grasp for air. I can't decide what is scaring me more, the thought of not waking up or lying here tormented. Hours go by and suddenly it's a new dawn, a new day, but no Nina, I don't feel good.

I Will

Ashley Crookall

Tell me you love me
I will run away
Try to break free
I will beg you to stay
Offer me your support
I will be out that door
Leave me be
I will be sobbing on the floor
Pull me in close
I will squirm in fear
Push me away
I will need you near
Tell me I am right
I will believe I am wrong
Tell me I am wanted
I will feel I don't belong
Tell me you are happy
I will tell you goodbye
Tell me it is over
I will crumble and cry
Lean in for a kiss
I will back down
Deny my embrace
I will curse and frown
Treat me like I matter
I will assume you don't care
Listen to my cruel words
I will tell you life is not fair
Tell me this is forever
I will guess we are done

Tell me it's not working
I will sneer 'this was just fun'
Tell me things are fine
I will tell myself they're not
Tell me you need space
I will plead; you're all I have got
Tell me the truth
I will insist it's a lie
Tell me you are done
I will feel my heart die

Rock Bottom

Ashley Crookall

I am incomplete
Insecure, no self-worth
Locked in my own skin

Exhilarating
Powerless over control
Destructive. Deadly

I am all consumed
Momentary release
Intoxicating

No spirit, no hope
I am weak, broken, alone
Destined self-destruct

Chaos, lust, ego;
Irrational hedonist
Slowly killing me

Where did it go wrong?
Numbing passion, price on life
Stubborn. Dreams to dust

Wrapped up in my fear
My pain, anguish, suffering
Why don't I belong?

Broken heart races
Crippling insomnia

Is this how it ends

Defiance, denial
Action without consequence
Survival, unknown

Know you are worth it
Take a chance. Be brave, fight, live
Stay strong. Stay strong. Stay.

Together We Can

Ashley Crookall

I have stolen more than I can ever repay
I have sold my dignity night and day
I have pawned my soul and suffered internal despair
I have learnt to fight back and have strength to repair

Friends around me stumble and fall
Terrified, to reach out and call
We unite; no better, no worse
Together we can manage this curse
Dark infiltrations of our minds
Yet we have the chance to survive

Through thick and thin, good and bad
Feelings of joy and those that are sad
There are ups and downs, losses and gains
But through supporting each other, we can remain

Turnaround

Ashley Crookall

Life can change, life can get better. It is possible to turn an internal trauma into a wonderful journey of discovering yourself and what your capabilities may be.

I arrived broken, a shell of a human. Numb, isolated and insistent my future would be bleak. Every step I took was a step too far, every person I met led to an uncomfortable conversation I would rather not have.

That was then. That in no way needs to define who I am today, what I can achieve and who I can become. With faith, with support and a level of trust, I have grown. I am different; I am slowly becoming a person who I need not fear. I no longer have to the hate the girl I was and can allow myself to embrace the woman I am becoming.

I have made mistakes, too many to count and some I am not ready to face but I know in time I can learn to accept my past and leave it behind, a distant memory.

I have welcomed the gift of chance. Grabbed hold of the opportunity I have been handed and count myself incredibly lucky to be where I am today. I could quite easily be in a very different place.

Aside from the realisation my manic lifestyle could have left me dead, I could have understandably and deservedly been locked away for the crime I committed.

Fortunately, there has been another option, an option I didn't believe was available to me, a way to rehabilitate myself in ways I could not understand, ways I thought I was not worthy of, nor thought would have any kind of profound effect on me.

By attending a facility, designed specifically for women, on a weekly basis my life has changed. I have welcomed help, shown my vulnerabilities and exposed some of my demons. I have come to terms with the fact I cannot change on my own and accept that people may actually care what happens to me.

The staff have all been a fantastic support; there is an aura of unity and a feeling of belonging. Encouragement is provided, and no judgment is apparent. It is a place that can provide hope for the desperate and a place where I have rebuilt myself slowly, taking each day at a time. It is not a place where you are locked away from your loved ones, unable to rebuild fractured relationships. It does not take that remaining bit of self-worth away from you. It is a safe environment.

I have attended various groups, engaged with other women, albeit some more ready for a better life than others, but their time will come, and the door will be open.

Boxing has provided me with the physical strength I have lacked for much of my life. It has given me the chance to engage with people and build up my confidence.

The drug awareness course has given me hope and clarity around my years of insanity and how I no longer have to live that way of life.

The creative writing course has inspired me and unearthed a passion deep inside of me that I never knew existed. It has been inspiring and allowed me freedom from myself and my inner darkest thoughts and memories.

Today I am grateful. It is a simple concept and the clue is in the title.

A Second Chance

Rebecca Gorman

110 Aigburth Road, Liverpool. A collection of ticking time capsules buried in a second chance. Swarming every corner eagle-eyed, hunting, pursuing, picturing the array of sweet interior nothings, illuminated in up-cycled chic. Glistening at the entrance, no bigger than a bag of sugar, suspended from plush velvet ribbon - a beaded veridian heart. My window-shopping soul sinks, like the sorrow of a singular magpie. Blinded in the chaos of so many mis-matching bizarre entities.

Background, bartering, banter. Bouncing of Her Majesty's mismatched tea sets. Nattering gaggles of ninnies exchanging pleasantries. Hipsters lolling at Instagram-able objects. A broad Toxteth tone murmurs 'that's three-pounds-fifty, brand new in Primark'. A local mum of three versus voluntary shop assistant. Both parties fighting a worthy cause over a frame of the finest cubic zirconia, while a fragrant millennial-musk echoes through peeling Acid-House T-shirts. Neither party backs down. A burst of nostalgia hits me during the delicate brawl, landing me in a vivid memory of my most valued transaction within this scrambled donation outlet.

A pair of black, Campbell knee-high moon-boots £6. An absolute steal. Although my heart was set on five. So, I began a negatively detailed examination of each scuff, scratch, or suspect indent from any prior relations. This visual interrogation of my soon-to-be boots ignited a financially themed tug of war with the very same, stern shop assistant.

Eventually our battle reaches a crescendo in a shared, sour purse of the lips, a cutthroat crossing of the arms, and a Marge-Simpson-like grunt. Frowning viciously, I wave my white six-pound flag, tail between my legs.

In retrospect, my intent to buy ended wholly justified in the soft crunchy winter snow of the Peak District, bouncing round like an infantile Neil Armstrong, my tucked-in-toes praised a truly-sound memory-foam investment.

Pennies hit the counter back in the jumbled reality of the pre-owned merchandise store. The mother-hen lost the battle and was now doomed to pay. I sauntered toward a blue Nestle milk crate of used frames. Bedazzled, bejewelled, beaming and caked in rainbow glitter. Ranging from an adorably affordable fifty-pence to five pounds worth of daylight-robbery, in a box resembling the vomit of a mythical creature. I dive loudly in to the sea of miscellaneous-memory fixtures.

Streaked upon a glass insert of pearlescent-steel mounting, while dancing in the hazy glow of a sunbeam, I catch a reflection. The beaded veridian heart, speaking in shimmering rays. Whispering, joking, teasing while toying with my decorative side. I debate an investment of the Queen's-gold once more. Still no avail, even with the intrigue of bohemian-flair in a collection of second chances.

Again, the nostalgic-allure of a hundred and ten Aigburth Road renders me unworthy of ownership and worthy only of subtle sensory appreciation. In a fortress of miscellaneous wonder. where everything has been held before, a collection of ticking time capsules.

Christopher Boffkin

Rebecca Gorman

With your curvy baby face, full with dense blonde curls
With your voice so solid against the right-wing con-artists
With your innocent blue eyes, dilated like dark pennies
With your top off, game on, in front of finely tuned sound system.
With your 'bail-eranos' ending your evenings, basking in back chat.
With your climbing efforts intrigued by the tallest trees of Denby
With your go-faster stripes painted upon a nineties red Nissan Micra
With your paying extra for those liner-marks on the insurance.
With your proud comfortable parents Alan and Gaynor broken
With your annoying little brother, whose life you helped shape
With your can't stop addicted to the shindig on rural Eastham roads
With your skiving lessons in sixth form to catch up on Willaston dreams
With your zephyr sized eyes pleased with over detailed illustrations
With your off the grain view locked in my mind forever, prepared for war
With your mess you left behind in your true essence; McCabe-shambles
With your partner in crime Pedro, who forever longs for your return
With your black and white checkered chef pants in multi-

coloured motion always
With your last words to me so lost, adrift solemnly introverted
With your words of wisdom knowing bitter tastes of Her Majesty's darkness
With your true essence of your character - a memory, at times hard to recall
With your swooning love for nature's winged-insects, no matter the size or scale
With your band of brothers, with you always, hoping to see your face thriving
With your being gone so long we force ourselves to remember
With your being alive, being so hard to forget

Saved Me

Rebecca Gorman

On the warm August concrete of Sandhills train station
A tearing, lower torso pain threw me to the ground
Clutching my gut like a ripping Tesco bag
I staggered toward the sea of lifts stairs and slopes
Forged in a chaotic labyrinth of Merseyrail-yellow

Through my tearing up tear ducts
My eyes clock the 1980's style information board
Hunts Cross - 2.51pm, expected 2.54pm. Fuck
Stunned to know if my pain threshold was willing to
Withstand such agonising and traumatic discomfort
I sit slanted on the platform curled up like a pretzel
Sweating, gasping, panting, praying for air

Welcome to the O2 messaging service
My headphones inform my beloved's unavailability
My only reliable life line, my only way home
Tense all over my pink fingers tied around my stomach
In the hope I'll wake up from this hellish nightmare

'Excuse me, do you need me to call an ambulance?'
Asks a kind concerned bystander in range of my despair
In silence I solemnly shake my head. 15 minutes later
After throwing around my giblets on a testing train journey
I scarper off with passengers glaring confused and curious
As to what may have caused my publicly noticeable affliction
I took a moment in all the pain to mentally thank every
Overly nice Scouse-nana, that asked me if I was alright?

As retro carriage slows down in a blur of a scenic motion
I see my knight on a white horse avidly checking his iPhone
The scream of brakes grinding to a halt. The tracks talk
As if they were the sound of my heart's own violin strings
For a second the pain stops, in sheer disbelief I pick myself up
And launch myself toward him, contented in his presence
immersed in his attendance, subdued to his splendour
Like a brand new bride after too many bouquets of blue bubbly
He scoops me into his grip while shuffling me off up platform
Gazing at him as he smooths his thumb across my cheeks
Brushing away the tears. I am whole. Questioning nothing
Safely within his arms

Turnaround

Rebecca Gorman

Bitter, brimming with confrontations, anger and frustration
I step to the enforced white gloss double doors
Soaked in a year's worth of brutal vendettas
Certain nothing could change me
I sat distant in my first session
Silent, teary and solemnly subdued
A puppet to a system I couldn't understand or control

Two sessions every week for ten to twelve weeks
At the beginning mentally broke me down
Midway building me back up. Ascending
Thoughts back to realistic splurges of playful
Purley for the sake of affirmations

At week eight my affirmations became real
Through good company, conversations and perseverance
Finding myself again felt easy
Much easier than before
I now know. For as long as I am on this earth
I am the most important person to me

Festival Fun Time

Rebecca Gorman

Thursday country miles
Executing months of talk
A-roads for the win

Rhubarb and Ginger
Featuring botanicals
Tents up, glug glug glug

Glare of rainbow swash
Grinning like a Cheshire cat
The rabbit hole smile.

Lie on mother earth
Only for a moment please
Reality ploy

Pulse, mic check one-two
Truly in the lion's mouth
Tested of my means

Bonded in amens
Primal vibration instinct
Feeding the rhyme

Roses, horns, tails,
Crows circle, burnt-out bass-lines
Running through Sunday

Monday blue
Who am I to say never?
Glamping with a view

Multicolour fiending for more

Who am I to say

Anticipation of Play

Rebecca Gorman

Collective thought
Unit hanging on a note
Niles' drums take control

Orchestrating tune
Eyes share, pushing ego
Pulsate now together

Fearing nothing more
A force to be reckoned with
tar like wax sings

Together count six
Mellifluous nature
Fluorescent funk tones

Malibu smoke tours
My dreams limitless larks
Expanding always

Compromise no sound
Obstruction to cause delay
Rife Meditation

Aims of tent events
Bunting, bubbles, bugles, sun
Triple-A surfing countries

Silence, one moment
Pure synchronisation looms
The Rhythm is next

Pipe-dreams need hard work
Perseverance is the key
To achieve Greatness

Otterspool

Rebecca Gorman

A die with three faces
Thorn pricked youths roll down hill
To Molotov chaos

The River Mersey
Salt, wind, mist. Dawn cries murder
Stray dogs' teeth run riot

Mound of emerald verge
Rolling, laughing, running free
In retrospect. Love

Red Hot Chilli's play
Seven seats of pungent noise
Unified in ore

Illness hidden pride
Smiles faded into dust
Your past makes you real

Good seeks out evil
Train tracks jaunt to stop jitters
Words enforce patience

Pack, seal, lock the house
New face, new place, new suit
The journey made me

Today a new day
Balance between the two still
In Molotov chaos

How Long?

Rebecca Gorman

Is it frayed at both ends maybe? In unimaginable proportions
A combination of thread from every colour swatch ever known
Possibly involved with flashes of glittery omnivalent twine

A statement piece immersed in decades of soundless talk
A known relic woven by the family of blind nuns praying for answers?
No holds barred every time, an array of unquantifiable proportions

A recurring halt in translation of speech. Inanimate it may be
My dad recites its predictable ways to me, as his mother did to him
Unpredictably illusive, constantly questionable. In my youth I was clueless

Personifying a solid backhanded statement; an incessant conversation ender
A robustly rhetorical poise, A neat stopping of words, Tied in an omnipotent bow
Agree to disagree at endless lengths, I ask? How long is a piece of string?

Inside the Magic Box

Rebecca Gorman

My box is made of chameleon skin
And inside my box is

Three starving Tamagotchis
Two aspiring singers bathing in falsified promise
One monochrome unicorn made of cake

And inside my box is

A gaggle of intoxicated chivalrous stags
Two kaleidoscopes of fluttering butterfly wings
A human ear desolate in a dark alley

I will put into the box

Three men with cerebral palsy
Two gothic cherubs with black wings
One conviction for the invisible man

I will keep safe in my box

Three distilled bottles of Missy Elliot's gin
Two industrial sized tin openers
One lost marble

My box hides away

Three severed torsos of soldiers
Two stoned hippies
One pungent smell of bacon

Woman

Rebecca Gorman

Me and women
We don't usually get along
Seeing myself as a Tomboy
Trainers, hoodies, bass music
Nike, Adidas thrills, Kappa laughs
Woman. Endlessly media-ised
Perfect skin, hair, body tattoos
No woman is perfect
No woman is truly a woman
If she doesn't find herself beautiful
In ever changing perspective of the world

The women in my life are solid
Mum, Nan, Sister, few friends cross country
I have no woman I call my best friend
Does that make me less of a woman?
As I appreciate them for no bond breaking
Dependence confided in pure love
Woman to me means being filled with
A strong sense of self-respect

Watching Them (Watching Me)

Dawn-Paisley Mills

You watch her, and she keeps watching you
Her thoughts keep the air turning blue
Betrothed is the sound that rings true
But who cares, she's besotted with you

You are there when she enters the court
Elegant, but still deeply in thought
'Hard-to-get' is the game she was taught
Other fish in that place to be caught

His green eyes, her black heart, they don't match
He's handsome, so cute, a fine catch
Win his heart, is a plan she must hatch
Lock the door, turn the key, move the latch

She is slim, she is tall, he's robust
Still her fire for him keeps on burning with lust
He has seen how they treat her unjust
He seeks justice for her, it's a must

On his side, it's so green as the grass
She admires his fine social class
But she can't seem to break through the glass
Poor Yorick! We knew him alas!

He has taken an oath for the truth
He approaches her - way too aloof
He keeps fighting for her, nail and tooth
Such passions flowing all under one roof

She can't eat, she can't sleep, she can't think
And she won't drown her sorrows in the demon drink
She can't eat, she can't sleep, she can't breathe
Please take her, I beg you, don't leave!

Rest in peace to the girl that you see
Kiss her once, say goodbye, abandon me!
Love is blind, this is true, she can't see
It will all end in tears quite possibly

Please take her hand, when you jump, are you scared?
In the courts their dirty laundry will be aired
Oh, my Adonis! To thee I shall compare!
Now the Judge, and the Lawyers, they all know you really cared

For all that is glitter, it is truly made of gold
She is arrogant and loud, she is bitter, she is bold
Narcissistic is the word that she's constantly been told
You like her style, please stay awhile, and the truth will soon unfold
They are liars, thieves and snakes and dirty dogs, and oh behold!

In her bed, he takes charge, it may seem
She's a hunger for him, just like strawberries and cream
And her skin feels like silk, bathing in milk, she is pristine
But when she woke up, it was only a dream

In the Courts, they both sit, side by side
And her love for this man, she must hide
Full of hate, full of love, filled with pride
Chemistry, passions and sparks all collide
Is this a match made in Heaven, or just suicide?

They embrace, they entwine, it may seem
Hot 'n' heavy in the lift, see the steam
Hot as hell, he's a manmade machine

It's 'Goin' down' if you know what I mean!
See her name on his back, hear her scream
See the bodies writhing on the CCTV screen
Now in The Ladies, it's divine intervene
They're a Dirty Double Act, they're a Team
As they enter the court, see her skirt, it's pristine
But all of these things, only happen in a dream

How long can she keep him alive?
And suppress her exploding sex drive
Just one kiss, just to help her survive
In his presence, please don't act like you're five

And if she only knew, only knew through it all
It was he who would certainly cause her to fall
Look at you now, you need someone to fall upon
You already knew that he was promised to someone
And in the next few days, he'll be gone, long gone
He was the object of her affection, he wasn't just anyone
She hears Marvin Gaye singing, 'Let's Get It On'
Now there's no date, there's no man, there's no ring, there's no prom.

But in reality, this is all so very wrong
And in the eyes of the Lord I have sinned, but for how long?
Just to succumb to him as well
Would you drag him down to hell?
In your dream of kiss and tell
You must release him, not deceive him, I pray tell

Everyone has his own cross to bear
And my behaviour, it seems, most unfair
And I don't really wanna take you there
I do apologise because I really do care!

Apocalypse Nursery Rhyme

Dawn-Paisley Mills

Fire fire burn
London Bridge is falling down
When will people learn?

Racing manic wild
Jack fell down and broke his crown
Every man and child

Jill came tumbling after
Silence Screaming from Her Mouth
Hear no more laughter

Running out of time
Hickory Dickory Dock
Let's commit a crime

Fetch a pail of gin
Burnt mice running down the clock
Hiding in the bin

Humpty by the road
He cannot even run fast
Then his guts explode

Hear the children cry
Georgy Porgy kiss the girls
Then they wave goodbye

All the king's horses
And all the king's men
Outnumbered by these forces

1 2 3 4 5
Look the sharks are burning up
Not one is alive

Sun is turning black
Once I caught a fish alive
Ground begins to crack

Bodies turning red
Old Macdonald had a farm
Now the pigs are dead

Ring a Ring o' Rose
A graveyard full of posies
All dead, I suppose

Burning in his car
Twinkle Twinkle Little Star
Never got that far

Hear the people scream
Row row row ya boat gently
Blood is in the stream

Systems overload
Puss In Boots is just a cat
Kermit's now a toad

Jack Spratt, just like that
Was killed without his wifey
Hanging with his hat

Old King Cole is dead
He had twenty thousand men
Merry in his bed

Sleeping in his bed
Was poor Wee Willy Winky
Now he's effin' dead

Hung drawn and quartered
Georgy Porgie Paedophile
Lynched burned and slaughtered

Armed guard now deployed
When the boys came out to play
Everything destroyed

1 2 3 4 5
No more people left alive
Six seven eight nine

Rock a Bye Babies!

Charity Shop Blues

Dawn-Paisley Mills

I'm going to the charity shop
And I ain't got time to stop
I got ten bags here, and a Zulu spear
A gold chain, and a lollipop

I'm going to a car boot sale
See a man, who's the size of a whale
Selling junk in his trunk, and a head like a monk
A red face, and a belly full of ale

Now I'm looking in the Red Cross gaff
It's full of shite, but I feel like a laugh
See a pram so stale, and a stuffed dog's tail
Earthquake, it's the aftermath!

Now I'm looking for a wedding dress
Oxfam is my next address
But I don't like the tag, or the matching handbag
And the bow on the back looks a mess!

Now a dead snake is still hissing
And a couple fornicate while kissing
So, take your bric a brac, and the plate with the crack
The dead cat with the eye missing

Old stock that's the size of the sea
We dedicate in the name of charity
While the years unfold, and a bra so old
It can't even hold a double-D!
The old woman in the charity shop
With the body that's ready for the chop!

Talking EastEnders, while a few offenders
Get her bag, and the money on top!

Fake legs, and ceramic elephants
Pink knickers and the scruffy underpants
Tommy Cooper on the shelf, it's Christmas day on the 12th
And a vase full of mouldy fake plants

Who the hell wants a dead man's briefs?
A container full of granny's old teeth
And a fucked-up fox, presented neatly in a box

Debt Collector

Dawn-Paisley Mills

Debt Collectors calling
Can you feel your heart rate falling
Have a heart attack, it's appalling
Now ya tearing out ya hair and a bawling

Debt Collectors sneaking
Can you hear your own voice, you're a shrieking
Going mad in the head, now ya streaking
Now your pissing down ya leg
You're a leaking

Debt Collectors creeping
See ya sitting in your room, you're a weeping
See the sweat across ya brow
It's a seeping
Now ya jumping on the bed
Like Five Lords a leaping

Hear the Debt Collector singing
Now ya listen for ya doorbell a ringing
Smell the sweat on ya body
You're a minging
Still the Debt Collector's noose keeps a swinging

HEY LIAR!

Dawn-Paisley Mills

Hear you twisting up the truth, and you conspire
You are empty, with no proof, your words are dire
Your lies they spread for miles and miles
And start a fire
Hopefully the truth will soon unravel, and transpire

HEY LIAR!
You're telling lies from here to there, and coast to coast
I have seen the evidence, inside my post
You go to hell, I hope you roast
Now you are maxing out your lies, you overdosed
Now for all the broken lives, let's drink a toast
Cos there's a liar in our midst, just like a ghost

HEY LIAR!
You see we enter through the front, and you the back
We are always on our guard, from your attack
It's a conscience and a life that you must lack
And there's no room for your knife inside my back
See the scars are firmly set, just like a track

HEY LIAR!
It's time to stop and see the truth before your eyes
I can hear the people weep, and babies' cries
You don't want to tell the truth, you are not wise
And every day that lies are spread and someone dies
You simply fail to show some grace and recognise

HEY LIAR!
Why don't you pack your bags, and please expire?
You are oral suicide, you never tire

So just close your lying mouth, and please retire
You're standing, watching, like a bird upon a wire
And your lies are causing victims to perspire

HEY LIAR!
You keep astounding, so profound, but can't you see
And you really bend the truth so naturally
And it's clearly damaging for all to see
Even demons do applaud you willingly
You twist the lies around your tongue from A to Zee
And you are covered in your own hypocrisy
You find it easy when you're criticising me
Now please go perfect your art below the sea, and get behind me

I’m Moving House Again

Dawn-Paisley Mills

And so I’m moving house again
I don’t care about the rain
I’ve only been here six months now
I’m trying hard to avoid a row
But I really don’t know how

And if I stay I will explode
And so, I’m moving from this road
My hatred’s such a heavy load
And now I’ve switched to moving mode

And so, I’m moving house once more
Don’t like the family from next door
They watch football, and shout ‘ENCORE!’
Their taste in music, I abhor
They’re banging drums, I can’t ignore
So, should I even up the score?
By dancing, stamping on the floor
The acoustics are hardcore
Should I abandon ship once more?

And now my children hear me shout
I hate this house, I must get out!
They’re throwing parties until two
What the hell am I to do?
I think I’ll practise my Voodoo

I’m hearing barking from the South
I’ll stuff a football in its mouth

The neighbour's dog just won't shut up
Now it's gone and had a pup
Now all my dreams they interrupt

Oh moving house I just adore!
From Hollywood to Singapore
Je'taime, j'adore, like Christmas day and so much more

I've left my neighbours all behind
To search and seek, and finally find
The perfect house I had in mind
It's made of gold, and all fur-lined!

Inside the Champagne Box

Dawn-Paisley Mills

My magic box contains champagne
And I have banned the word called Pain
And introduced the word Insane
They say my crime is I'm too vain!

My five children re-appeared
And the Guardian disappeared
And the Judge was found all speared
It was just as they had feared!

Old ladies with white teeth, and the generous thief
And when the babies die, there is no longer any grief
And on mischievous night, there ain't no sign of any mischief!

The chocolate tastes like gravy, and the waves no longer wavy
Dave Dee Micky Titch and Davy!

And the ocean lies quite still, death is not a bitter pill
And no land is to be conquered, and there is no pure self will
Please show mercy when you kill!

Dinosaurs have skin like silk, blood-red flowing from breast milk
Just like cabbages and kings, let's wear ten engagement rings
I don't know why the caged bird sings?

Because I think of other things
I don't feel like being kissed, but I feel like getting pissed
I hear the Judge say 'Case dismissed!'
Crack-cocaine I can't resist, I'm rising through the red red mist

I throw my money in the air, and I shave off all my hair
'Shall I compare me to a Summer's night' 'I am more lovely, and more fair!

'Oh, I never speak my mind'
My mouth is pure and all fur-lined, the truth is never hard to find
I'm never good, I'm never kind, hate-mail always should be signed!
Still you stab me and I smile, I can run a minute mile
I'm telling lies, I'm not tactile, new-born babies are so vile!

Climb inside my box, my shroud, enjoy my ice-cream covered cloud
I killed a man, I feel quite proud, taking kids is not allowed
And they won't stop telling me, that I'm detached from reality!

The Money

Dawn-Paisley Mills

A shiny black sports car screeched to a halt in the middle of the street and two hardened criminals got out and ran into a nearby garden with opened patio doors. A tied-up, snarling black dog dived viciously towards them but was sent sprawling on its back from a kick to the ribs from a hundred-mile-per-hour, black hobnail boot. Its painful yelp could be heard all the way down the street.

Diane arrived home to be greeted by a pile of bills on the hallway mat. A tall slim woman with long red hair, tied back tightly in a ponytail. She was tired, and her feet hurt from standing and walking all day looking for jobs. She didn't have the guts to tell her husband that she'd lost her job the week before after challenging her boss about a pay rise and extra hours. After threats and insults were made, Diane was fired from her job.

She walked towards the kitchen and threw the unopened bills down on the table and went quickly to the opened kitchen window to close it, as her neighbour's dog yelped and barked. As she turned to sit at the table, she noticed a black bin liner on the edge of the kitchen table, tied in a knot.

At first Diane did not want to touch the black bin liner and took a step backwards, fearful for a few moments while she tried to figure out why a black bin liner would be on her dining table, that wasn't there when she left the house in the morning. She grabbed a huge carving knife and began to prod and poke at the suspect baggage. Eventually curiosity got the better of her and the carving knife had reassured her that the contents of the bin liner was safe enough to open and investigate. Still stabbing at the bag and half opening it with the other hand, while standing at a safe distance, eventually the bag tore and several wads of money were revealed. Diane's eyes widened as she tore open the rest of the bag, her heart racing with fear and absolute joy.

She quickly ran to the kitchen windows and drew all the blinds while scanning nervously for any onlookers. Her breathing was fast, and she knocked over a glass in her haste to conceal her find. She then scooped up all the money, drawing the pile of money tightly towards her double-D breasts, and ran quickly upstairs to her bedroom, stumbling up the first three steps with excitement and fear at her discovery on the kitchen table.

Two streets away in a dark, cold cellar, two burly, red-faced men nearly came to blows as they argued and exchanged insults about who was responsible for their plans going wrong. Spit flying and frothing at the mouth, both men shouted angrily at each other, enraged, their veins pulsating from their temples and thick necks. One shouted 'This is your fault!' 'Now the pigs are on to us,' the other one replied. 'You did this ya useless bastard - you took too long' and then he grabbed a gun and held it dangerously to the other man's head. 'Say one more word and I'll kill ya.' 'Go on! I dare ya.' The other man froze for a few seconds and kept still, then without warning he managed to grab the gun that was so close to his head, and both men wrestled each other to the ground. The gun was sent flying in to a far corner of the cellar as both of the men raced to recover possession and control.

One of the men struggled free of the other's tight, powerful grasp and crawled on his knees quickly towards the gun, dishing out a powerful back-kick to the other man's head as he would not let go and held on tight. A loud bang echoed around the cellar and the awful sound of choking, gurgling and gasping for breath could be heard until it eventually stopped. The strong smell of iron and a thick pool of dark blood now spread rapidly across the cold cellar floor.

Diane's husband, an electrician, and two teenage sons had now arrived home from Art College. She surprised them at the front door with a huge bottle of Champagne and kissed and hugged them all and said she was taking them out to an Italian restaurant to celebrate a pay rise at work and that they had to pack a bag because she had booked them all in to an expensive hotel for the night. Her parents would be staying over for the night to watch the house. A black private taxi arrived for the happy family of four as they climbed in, chatting excitedly about the night ahead. Diane promised the boys a holiday and her husband a new car. He hugged and kissed her and said 'Well done, luv.'

Later on, at midnight, a huge dark figure went unnoticed breaking into a house, breaking the glass quietly with a towel wrapped around his powerful fist and climbing through a window. The fierce black dog that lived next door was unusually quiet and the moon disappeared. The large figure crept upstairs, entered a bedroom and switched on the lights. Looking under the bed he recovered an empty black bin liner, shredded and torn. He became agitated and infuriated as he upturned the bedroom looking for the bag's contents and found nothing.

Angered he stormed to the next bedroom and saw two figures fast asleep. He violently shook both the sleeping figures awake, ranting and shouting angrily: 'Where's the money? 'Where's the effin' money?'. The two scared figures froze in fear, unable to speak, and in shock from the presence of the huge fierce intruder. Two loud bangs could be heard, then there was a silence… The intruder left empty handed.

The Rain

Dawn-Paisley Mills

I love it when it rains
It takes away the pains

It brings a gentle calm
Reassuring gentle arm

I lie awake, and I can dream
My world of rain, my own sunbeam

It takes me to a different place
And all bad thoughts I can erase

It lies me down, and rocks to sleep
And lovers kiss, and gifts to keep

It holds me when I'm truly sad
And brings me peace I've never had

I summon rain, as if I'm God
But I don't have a staff or rod

I'm hoping that he hears my pain
And sends the rain down once again!

The Blue Shoes

Dawn-Paisley Mills

Six beautiful raven-haired sisters called Brenda, Billy, Belle, Bella, Beverly and little Bonnie lived in a cottage with their mum. Their father had died the year before and times were hard with no money available. He had left a small inheritance but most of that money was used to fix the leaky roof of the thatched cottage they lived in.

One day, the youngest, Bonnie, walked to the village shops and saw a pair of blue sequined shoes in a shop window. She loved them. Bonnie entered the shop and tried on the sparkly blue shoes, then admired herself in the mirror. She was a beautiful sight, spinning around with her long black hair and bright blue eyes, and the blue sequined shoes complemented her nicely.

The eldest of the six sisters had a birthday coming up in the next few days, and unbeknown to Bonnie, her mother had purchased the blue sequined shoes with the last of their inheritance money and a promise of two-dozen eggs every week to the shoe shop owner as part payment. Their father had reared chickens and would sell their eggs before he passed away.

When Monday arrived they all wished their eldest sister Brenda 'happy birthday', and she was presented with a blue box, wrapped up with a beautiful blue bow. Brenda opened the box and the glee shone on her face at the sight of such a beautiful pair of blue, sparkly sequined shoes. Bonnie on the other hand felt disappointment, hatred and sadness to see her beloved blue shoes being given to her eldest sister.

As the years went by, the blue sequined shoes were slowly passed down to each of the sisters, as the others grew out of them. The blue sequined shoes had been worn to a prom, a dinner date, a birthday party, the village disco, a wedding and a school Christmas party. Each sister had certainly enjoyed themselves and enjoyed wearing the gorgeous blue shoes.

Eventually the shoes were given to Bonnie, worn out, worn down, and some of the blue sequins were missing. The front of the shoes were scuffed and thread bare, and resembled nothing like the original brightly coloured, glossy, twinkly shoes that she had once seen in the shop window. She tried them on anyway, and they were too tight!

Can We Talk?

Dawn-Paisley Mills

Can we talk?
I've got something to say
Why have my children gone away?

Can we talk?
Because I'd really like to know
Where do all the absent fathers go?

Can we talk?
Because I've really had enough!
How can we take the smooth, with the rough?

Can we talk?
I don't really understand
Why nobody comes to hold my hand?

Can we talk?
About the things that I've seen
Can you hear me, where have you been?

Can we talk?
Can you see my body fade?
My peace of mind has been delayed!

Can we talk?
About what you did
You did those things, and then you hid!

Can we talk?
About my feelings again
That I find comfort in the pouring rain

Can we talk?
About your hatred of me
Your envy is not hard to see

Can we talk?
About burdens and miles
I'm finding it hard, to face all of my trials

Can we talk?
My silence, my tears
And how I can challenge all of my fears

I've decided, I don't want to talk!

Turn Around

J.B.

Turn your life around and have a second chance. Sounds wonderful and hopes rise high.

If only it could work. If only I could remove these labels. Strange how they stick. One for every path I try to take. One for every move I try to take.

There it is, the label that's meant to block me. The ones they pile high to make sure their weight holds me back. So, I could be called cynical. But turning around with labels pushing me down and encasing me is not something I can easily visualise.

Hopefully it's the start of something good. Maybe, just maybe, it will deliver its promise. Or maybe it will be stopped and become just another label.

Prison

J.B.

There are many preconceptions of women's prisons, all of which are rapidly dispelled within hours of actually being in one. My personal vision was one of orange jump-suited women wielding heroin filled syringes at the ready to greet me. The bad girl image of the television portrayal weighed heavy on me as I travelled in the filthy urine-smelling prison van with its tinted plastic windows and tiny plastic cells. It was a vision so terrifying, and I'm sure universal, that had been ingrained into the general public as a convenient spin to not only stop us from offending, but also to make sure we cared little as to what goes on behind the walls to the 'fallen women' held within them.

I'm making no excuses for the criminal actions of the women who find themselves at the mercy of the prison service; but whilst I met women who I sincerely believe should never be released I met many many more who should never have found themselves incarcerated. Not just for the pettiness of the crimes that kicked off their prison habit, but for the subsequently devastating effect that it has on not only their own lives but that of the children and family they left behind.

Generations of resentment towards authority naturally follow when a child sees the state lock up their mother. Many of these children then find their lives slide into a chaotic series of devastating consequences associated with the loss of a mother. Unfortunately, they are afforded little compassion, indeed they often go on to lose their homes, be shunted from one foster family to another and can easily lose touch with their extended family as well as their friends. Basically, their lives are devastated, and they very often go on to become offenders themselves. I still find it hard to rationalise that women who are unable to ensure their children attend school find themselves in custody. What chance does that child have of attending school with no mother at home?

In the time I subsequently spent in custody, I rarely met a woman who didn't have a tragic back story that led to her offending behaviour. Whilst it is easy and maybe reasonable to say not all victims of tragedy end up breaking the law, it is a platitude intended to steer us away from the compassion that could be afforded to these women, who may have been so broken by their lot that the strength and support that most of us can summon up without effort is simply not there for them. Mental illness, abuse, domestic violence on a scale most of us could not even imagine, and bereavements are the prevailing factors behind almost every woman that finds herself in prison.

Women suffer worse than men in the Criminal Justice System. Not only do they often receive longer sentences than men for similar crimes, they have a much higher chance of losing their children, their homes, as well as all their possessions, and are more likely to be shunned by extended families, public opinion and indeed the press.

Sarah's Story

J.B.

Sarah walked slowly up the leafy avenue, savouring every minute spent in the fresh sweet-smelling air. She took in every sight, sound and smell as she walked and thought of the contrast to the ones she usually encountered - arguments, screams and odours so foul the urge to vomit was never far away.

But for now she was free, movement pass in hand and full of the excitement and anticipation a visit to reception to pick up a parcel could bring. She imagined this was how children felt on the walk downstairs on Christmas morning. She'd never had that experience; her mother was never sober or drug-free long enough, but she'd seen it often enough on all the lovely Christmas films she'd watched over and over as a child. She'd never felt the loneliness of being on her own when she watched all the happy normal families enjoying the festive season with their families, gifts and endless food. Strangely she never felt self-pity, but instead had let herself become a part of the families in the films as she watched eagerly, becoming involved in them rather than just an observer. It was her coping mechanism, she supposed, as she thought back, and she remembered how she'd dreamed and indeed expected that her life would one day become like the ones she'd watched. When she grew up she was going to work hard, meet the man of her dreams and start the fairy tale life she knew was waiting round the corner for her. She'd fed her dream the only way she could, by reading wonderful novels and beautiful poetry that whisked her out of the reality of her situation and filled her with hope and excitement for the future that awaited her.

She'd almost started on the path to the life she'd longed for when she was thirteen. Her nan and granddad had fought against her mother and taken her to live with them and it was the closest thing to heaven Sarah had ever known. She'd been a part of a family and had meals, clean clothes, a warm bed and even went to school every day, something she'd never managed due to looking after her mother every hour of the day, as well as the dread of what she'd come home to if she did manage to go.

But it had been short lived. Her mum had turned up at the school gates one day and taken her to a new home 50 miles away where her nanna wouldn't know how to find her. Things had gone from bad to worse as they'd moved in with a man her mother had met, and Sarah felt a shiver run through her at the memory. She knew that was the start of her dreams becoming nightmares. The start of her childhood being taken away and replaced by an endless search for oblivion from the torture and abuse she was to endure. But worse than this was the guilt. Her mother blamed her for the nightly visits her new boyfriend made to her daughter, and in her drunken drug-addled state she failed to put a stop to his endless stream of friends that came round to take part in the abuse. She also blamed her for becoming hooked on the drugs these abusers had fed her when they became the only way to block out the pain of it all. Now she lived with the guilt of leaving her alone, having been sentenced for the crimes she'd committed in an attempt to feed her addiction.

The judge had told her she was a menace to society that needed locking away, so she supposed her mother was right - it was all her fault. She'd somehow been to blame for everything that had happened, so she rightly hated herself for it and she would make sure she'd cut herself extra deeply when she returned to her cell from reception.

But for now, she had a parcel from her Nan waiting for her - and who knows what wonderful gift it contained.

Second Time Around

J.B.

A wedding dress of beads and lace, destined to make another bride shine
Sat next to a teddy with wellington boots and a dogeared copy of the story of wine
A tired little tea-set that's seen better days,
A guide to cook potatoes fifty different ways
Designer clothes, last season's best.
My favourite team's last-season vest
A crate crammed with pottery, I wonder if it's hiding a piece of Clarice Cliff
A porcelain tree, a lamp made from shells,
A Christmas tree furnished with baubles and bells
All with a wealth of their memories untold,
Sit waiting for their new life to unfold

Autumn

J.B.

Autumn
Winter round the corner
Darker nights the curtains closed
Goodbye summer sun
Coats buttoned on walks
Boots that kick the leaves away
Grinding underfoot
Jack frost nipping toes
Flowers now bowing their heads
Resting now till spring
Writing Christmas lists
Getting the pumpkin ready
We love Halloween
Bonfire night comes next
The smell of fire and rockets
Watch them light the sky

Heart Beat

Karen Richards

Sound of water in the distance
Early morning on the beach
As the sun kisses my feet

Sunrise and sunset
All my favourite pictures
This is where I hear my heart beat

Lost In My Emotions

Linda Meshan

Lost in my mind
Overwhelming emotions
Too many to count
Pain
Sadness
Hurt
Confusion
Loss
What do I do?
What did I do?
A friend, a confidant, someone to talk to
Two weeks
Three years
I am lost

Billy and the Magic Pebble

Veronica Doyle

There was once a little boy named Billy. Nine years of age. He was on the beach one day with his mum and dad, making sand castles, but he was getting bored with them. He was thinking 'What if something magical happened? Then I would wish for everything I want…'

Then he saw a shiny pebble, he picked it up and said 'What if I could be somewhere else with this pebble? Oh, how I wish you were magic!' The pebble replied, 'What would you wish for Billy?' Billy got the fright of his life, 'Oh you are magic!'

It began to rain, Billy said, 'I hate the rain, I wish I was in a chocolate factory.' All of a sudden, he was flying through the air. Billy was terrified. Suddenly, he saw a slide… he was on it and sliding down it when he saw mountains of chocolate.

Billy was delighted: 'My dream has come true!' He tasted all the different kinds of chocolate, then he said 'What if I was in a candy store?'

He flew through the air. This time he wasn't scared. I know where I am going! he thought and was in the candy store, delightedly eating all different types of candy. 'I feel a bit sick,' said Billy - not knowing that the magic pebble was thinking, 'What a greedy little boy!'

'What if I were in a toy shop?' exclaimed Billy. There was a big gust of wind and the pebble announced, 'You can go to the toy shop if you are not greedy.' Billy was shocked, 'You can talk, I didn't know pebbles could talk.' The pebble replied, 'Only magic ones can talk.'

Billy was suddenly in a toy store, amazed at all the toys. 'I want all of these toys and I am going to have them.' The magic pebble was angry, 'No, you are not, you are not getting a thing!' Billy screamed 'I am, I am, I hate you magic pebble.' And with that Billy was back on the beach and the magic pebble was out of reach waiting for another little boy or girl. One who wasn't greedy but in need for some magic in their life.

Billy was still screaming 'I hate that magic pebble,' and he was back on the beach with his family. They said, 'What are you talking about?' He told them all about the magic pebble and the chocolate factory and candy store and the toy shop. They said 'Billy, don't be silly, you have been nowhere'.

The magic pebble was going, 'Ha ha ha, Silly Billy'.

Ninny

Veronica Doyle

It is Saturday night, a few of the grand-kids are in our Ninny's. All of the aunties and uncles are in the pub at the corner of the street. I say, 'Ninny is there jars out tonight?' 'Yeah, there is.'

She is making cheese and crackers, some sarnies, and a pan of bacon ribs is on the stove. She is going to the pub soon. One of my uncles walks in with loads of packets of crisps and little bottles of lemo, we are made up. She says, 'Don't have them crisps everywhere, put them there on the table till after.' Then she is off to the pub. She still has her pinny on. 'You lot be good till we come back, we won't be late. Jack will mind you.' Jack was the dog, he minded us.

As soon as the door was shut one of my cousins got on the piano. We were all singing and so was Jack, we were saying, 'Sing Jack!' and he was barking. We had a good time, we ate our crisps and had our lemo and in no time at all they were back from the pub carrying crates of beer. Everyone gave a cheer. 'The ale is here!' my Ninny said. 'Jars out. No scouse on the house tonight, I have got a big pan of ribs on.'

One of my uncles said, 'Ma get the spoons out and the tin ash tray and the wash board.' It was a great time in my Ninny's in those days! One Uncle playing the spoons, one playing the ash tray with a penny, one on the piano and one on the wash board. Everyone singing and dancing.

We ate all the ribs, sarnies and cheese and crackers. It was getting late, time to go home. Ninny shouted, 'Close that gate.' I said, 'Nin I will be over tomorrow after church for my treat.' She said, 'Okay queen, Goodnight. God bless.'

The next day I walked in and there on the table was a ham shank and a bottle of Camp coffee. Ninny said, 'Where have you been Queen?' Here's your shank-butty and your cup of Camp coffee.' It was lovely. Nothing like your ninny's shank butty and coffee. When I was finally going home, she said, 'There you go. Some toffee to eat on the way home.' 'Thanks Ninny, see you soon'.

Broken Doll

Veronica Doyle

I was riding on my bike one day with my friends. I had my doll, Jill, with me. We were riding very fast, but I still came last because I fell off my bike and my doll Jill went rolling down the hill.

Someone said, 'Jill will be ok, just give her a pill.' And we went back up the hill to go home to my mam (who will moan).

My poor broken doll Jill!

I am going to put her in my magic box so the sly-fox won't get her. I will seal it with magic dust and golden ribbon so that it won't get any rust. We will go up the big mountain and get a drink of the magic water that comes out of a fountain,

I lie on top of that mountain and go to sleep, I dream I can hear the running of the water and bright colours dancing all around. Then my magic box opens, and my broken doll Jill gets out and she starts to dance! I think 'I am in a trance! That can't be my Jill, she is broken!'

I wake up quick. My mam says, 'Come on, it's time for school.'

It was only a dream, Jill was asleep on my pillow with her gingham dress on…

Oxfam

Veronica Doyle

I am looking in the window of an Oxfam shop. I see a red hula hoop, the same one I had under the bed when I was little for 50p. Then I see a child's coat for £2. It is old - but the bold colours! It is magical.

Someone gave it away - must have been nice in its day. Did the child cry when it was given away? Day after day I am thinking what is the story behind it? Did they lose it, and somebody found it?

Kitchen Table

Veronica Doyle

Mary walks in the kitchen after her long day in work. She could not wait for her tea, she was hungry. Hope my mam has left me something nice to eat. She walks in, turns the light on and there on the table…

Wait for it…

… is a BIG LION growling at her.

Mary takes to her heels and runs away screaming.

The Wrong Shoes

Veronica Doyle

Mam said, 'Come on Veronica I am taking you for new shoes.' I was made-up, thinking, 'I know what shoes I want!'

They had a little heel on them. They were a lovely shade of red.

We got to the shop and I said, 'Mam! There they are!' She said, 'You're not getting them, Only fallen women wear them!'

She dragged me over to another shop and bought me a horrible black pair, I hated them! Then we got the bus home. I was sulking as we got off the bus but I'd left those black shoes on the seat on purpose…

I had a sly smile on my face. Good! I was NEVER going to wear them.

Storm Clouds

Veronica Doyle

We moved to our flat in the sixties: it was called the slum clearance.

We loved our house in Great Homer Street. All the neighbours looked after one another. We moved to a flat on the fourteenth floor, my mam loved it! The view was great and we had a bathroom and a toilet. In our old house we had a tin bath and the toilet was in the backyard.

I was never scared of thunder and lightning. In our house I would look out of the window at it. My brother was scared of it, he would run upstairs and hide under the bed. We would laugh at him. My mam would turn all the mirrors around, she would say don't touch the knives and forks and turn the telly off,

My brother said, 'What if it thunders?' Mam said, 'Hide in the bathroom.' We all laughed, but he said, 'It's not funny!' One night I was in bed asleep and my brother was going, 'Wake up, wake up,' I said 'Why?' He said, 'It's thunder and lightning!' I said, 'What have you woken me up for?' He said, 'It is bad, I have never seen it like that!'

I got up. My mam said, 'O Girl, it is like the war! You would think the bombs were dropping!' I walk into the living room. We were on the fourteenth floor and our whole flat lit up. It was terrifying.

The caretaker of the flats came around asking if everyone was okay. We all crowded onto the staircase of the flats. Everyone was on them. It was really scary and some of the kids were crying. It went on all night long till about six in the morning. I don't think anyone went to school or work that day, and ever since that night I have been scared of thunder. We were in the flats for twenty-three years and all of that time I was scared of storms.

When we moved out of the flats to our house I thought I wouldn't be scared but I am. Ever since, if it's been thunder and lightning, I would run under the stairs in the cupboard and our dog would be behind me.

If only my brother hadn't woken me up all those years ago! I wouldn't be scared of storms.

Tiny Baby, Such a Joy

Paula Lee

Tiny baby, such a joy
Sweet angelic little boy
Lent to us from God above
But love we did with all our heart
It hurts so much to have to part
But now it's time to say goodbye
Be not ashamed if you should cry
Because we had him for a time
When he was yours and he was mine

Love Shared

Paula Lee

Sound of air bubble popping in mist
Our wrigglies have done their work
Grey, dark speckled friend came near
To our delight
Slippery wet hooked-up friend
Slipped into our landing net
He's soon returned to wavy, silver rippling waves
Suddenly, current waves became alive
Wind gushing, rustling, came louder
From one smile to another in the beautiful moment
Our night began to drift, and dawn arisen
Our work was shared loving night
Love shared, between
Mum fights, where is my tights

Tea Time Rush

Paula Lee

Sweet tea time rush
Tea flask on the go
Rollies on, to and fro
Grandad's cap on, eyes down
As night falls here we go
Out came those little deckies
Out came them wrigglies
Fighting, waiting, shoving, pushing
Hey, hanging on the pole
Wind whistling, rustling in the trees
Beautiful waves slithering over the silver water
Ripples swirl into a slow twister.

What A Sight

Paula Lee

Summer holidays draw near, lots of exciting activities. A sunny morning, bright and early, ready and raring to go! Fights begin, bathroom big race, who's washed and dressed first.

Mum flapping frantically, constantly shouting, 'Jimmy, have you got the car loaded yet?' Suitcases getting passed down in a row between all five kids in a line, then us all five kids seated in the car, all excited.

Mum shouts, 'Jim, we got everything?'

'Yes, love. Just lock up now, love.'

Mum shuts the door, off on our big adventure.

Our five voices in the car after forty-five minutes, 'Are we there yet?' Reply: 'Not long.'

Twenty minutes later, 'Are we there yet?'

Before our eyes blinked we could smell those salty, breezy waves of the sea.

'Umm, can you smell onions, burgers, sweet buttery popcorn. Umm, candy floss, cherry red sticky lollipops.'

We get into our luxurious eight-berth caravan. Mum's unpacking suitcases, 'Jim, where's the carry bag?'

Dad says, 'It's there, love.'

'Oh great, I've got no bloody bloomers for tonight!'

Dad says, 'I've got an idea! Here, put these on! Put some bows or tie string around them wet Speedos.' 'Ah well, come on, let's go to the club.'

Wow! Disco lights, disco ball. Music blaring the great 80's, rock, roll, dance and beat the competition. Mum, Dad, rocking, rolling, swinging, jiving, Mum stumbles and us five kids had belly laughs and chuckles. Mum's panties,…oh no… Speedos, down by her ankles.

Night had drawn, music down, lights off, five sleepy kids, it's bed time.

That alarm bell, 8:00am. Us 'Bisto-kids' smelt breakfast, and gathered around the round table. Caravan door open as there's a heatwave inside. The fan blowing as we all stared at it to see Mum's bloomers on top.

What a sight for sore eyes!

Brandon Scott Southwell Lee

Paula Lee

D.O.B.: 08.10.97
Passed Away: 28.11.97

I would like to say a few words about our Brandon.

How very special a person he was. His smile would light up the room and, in every way, he was perfect from head to toe. I knew from the beginning that he was going to be a boy by the way he kicked, even at the early times; I'm sure he was dreaming of scoring a goal.

My family envisaged that he would support Everton, but, deep down, I knew he eventually would follow his father's footsteps, and support Liverpool.

I wondered who he would look like? Whose eyes, whose nose, whose mouth would he have? Would he take after Scott? Would he take after me?

The answer is neither; he looked like Brandon. He was, and is, a unique person. Shared by all the family, friends, and sisters on earth. And I'm sure that the little bud that was Brandon will grow, bloom, and be looked after by all up in Heaven above.

Love you always, Son.
Be missed ever so much.
Love,
Mum & Dad
xx

Our Morning Chorus

Tracy Jennings

The day starts at 7am, with the shouting, are you up yet
Hurry up, hurry up, hurry up
Then it starts, loud thuds on the floor as we scramble out of bed
The race is on to see if you can get the bathroom first, six shoving and pushing, the bickering is getting louder
The race is on to get dressed hoping that you are the one, who gets those matching socks
Mum is still shouting 'hurry up, hurry up, hurry up'
Breakfast is ready, and we scramble to be first, no one wants to be last
Mum still shouting hurry up, hurry up, hurry up
Breakfast is now finished, and we go another race to school, with that constant sound of mum shouting 'Hurry up hurry up, hurry up.'
To think we will do it all again tomorrow

The Turmoil

Tracy Jennings

The Turmoil is my mind, the noise inside is deafening
I try to escape it
It gets louder and louder
My hands sweat, yet I'm cold
The thoughts are twisting and turning, round and round they go
How do I escape
My thoughts are dark yet it's light
Please, please stop, I can't take it anymore

How Do I Fit

Tracy Jennings

A day with my anxiety, fantasising of being like everyone
else
I watch and listen
I wonder why I don't fit
The laughter is deafening, I feel uneasy
I shy away as my heart pounds
My thoughts are racing, I am breathless
I ask myself why can't they hear me
I am screaming inside
I feel alone

The Blue Eyes

Tracy Jennings

The blue eyes are heavy
Lead weights they feel
But the twitch
They settle darkness is here

My Mind

Tracy Jennings

A storm in a teacup, swirling round and round
It twists and turns
Please be still, be still

The View

Tracy Jennings

The view is vast and great
Everything big and small, bright and dark
Calm, I absorb the view

The Sound

Tracy Jennings

The sound wakes me
Bang, bang, flash, flash, bang, bang
That battering on the window

It's Here

Tracy Jennings

The excitement, I can't cope
My heart pounds as loud as a drum
Faster, faster here I come
Racing down the stairs
I can't catch my breath
Opening that door
Screams with excitement

Congratulations to all those who participated in *No Offence* for producing such quality writing and being generous enough to share their stories with us.

Writing on the Wall is a dynamic, Liverpool-based community organisation that celebrates writing in all its forms. We hold an annual festival and a series of year-round projects. We work with a broad and inclusive definition of writing that embraces literature, creative writing, journalism and nonfiction, poetry, song-writing, and storytelling. We work with local, national and international writers whose work provokes controversy and debate, and with all of Liverpool's communities to promote and celebrate individual and collective creativity. WoW creative writing projects support health, wellbeing and personal development.

If you have a story to tell, or would like to take part in, or work with WoW to develop a writing project, please get in touch – we'd love to hear from you.

Mike Morris and Madeline Heneghan, Co-Directors

info@writingonthewall.org.uk
www.writingonthewall.org.uk
0151 703 0020
@wowfest